The Don't Laugh Challenge™

SIBLING EDITION

Don’t Laugh Challenge BONUS PLAY

Join our Joke Club and get the Bonus Play PDF!

Simply send us an email to:

- **10 BONUS hilarious jokes for you and your sibling!**
- **An entry in our Monthly Giveaway of a $25 Amazon Gift card!**

We draw a new winner each month and will contact you via email!

Good luck!

Welcome to The Don't Laugh Challenge™

• How do you play?

The Don't Laugh Challenge is made up of 10 rounds with 2 games in each round. It is a 2-3 player game with the players being 'Goober #1','Goober #2', and a 'King' or 'Queen'. In each game you have an opportunity to score points by making the other players laugh.

After completing each round, tally up the points to determine the Round Champion! Add all 10 rounds together to see who is the Ultimate Don't Laugh Challenge Master! If you end up in a tie, use our final Tie Breaker Round for a Winner Takes All!

• Who can play the game?

Get the whole family involved! Grab a family member or a friend and take turns going back and forth. We've also added Bonus Points in game 2, so grab a 3rd person, a.k.a 'King' or 'Queen', and earn an extra point by making them guess your scene!

The Don't Laugh Challenge™ Activity Rules

- ## Game 1 - Jokes (1 point each)

Goober #1 will hold the book and read each joke to Goober #2. If the joke makes Goober #2 laugh, Goober #1 can record a point for the joke. Each joke is worth 1 point. At the end of the jokes, tally up your total Joke Points scored for Goober #1 and continue to Game 2!

- ## Game 2 - Silly Scenarios (2 points each + bonus point)

Without telling the other Goober what the scenarios say, read each scenario to yourself and then get creative by acting it out! You can use sound effects, but be sure not to say any words! If you make the other Goober laugh, record your points and continue to the next scenario.

BONUS POINT: Get your parents or a third player, a.k.a King or Queen, involved and have them guess what in the world you are doing! Get the King or Queen to guess the scene correctly and you score a BONUS POINT!

The Don't Laugh Challenge™ Activity Rules

Once Goober #1 completes both games it is Goober #2's turn. The directions at the bottom of the book will tell you who goes next. Once you have both completed all the games in the round, add your total points from each game to the Round Score Page and record the Round winner!

- ## How do you get started?

Flip a coin. If guessed correctly, then that Goober begins!

Tip: Make any of the activities extra funny by using facial expressions, funny voices or silly movements!

ROUND 1

Jokes

Who is a geologist's favorite wrestler?

The Rock.

/1

Did you know that I have met Bambi in real life? He's actually a deer friend of mine.

/1

Why is the bodybuilder such a good motivator?

He says things are always working out!

/1

Why were the two cows so sad when they were separated?

/1

They missed one an-udder.

JOKES TOTAL: /4

GOOBER 1 CONTINUE TO THE NEXT PAGE →

Silly Scenarios

(Act it out!)

You are a master chef preparing food, but you accidentally cut way too many onions. Here come the waterworks! Waaahhhh!

_____ /2

You are an evil witch concocting a fatal potion. Stirring vigorously, the mixture splashes on you and you begin to dramatically melt into a gigantic bubbling puddle!

_____ /2

SILLY SCENARIOS TOTAL: _____ /4

NOW, PASS THE BOOK TO GOOBER 2 →

Jokes

What is a basketball player's favorite place to eat?

DUNKIN' Donuts!

____ /1

What do you call a spaceship made from Coca-Cola containers?

A Bottle Rocket!

____ /1

Why is the bike so honest?

He likes to keep it wheel.

____ /1

What is a tornado's favorite party game?

Twister!

____ /1

JOKES TOTAL: ____ /4

GOOBER 2 CONTINUE TO THE NEXT PAGE →

Silly Scenarios

(Act it out!)

It's your turn to bowl! As you get ready, you accidentally cross the line and step into the super slippery lane! Pretend to lose your balance as you slip and slide all the way to the pins, and get a STRIKE!

_____ /2

It's a super windy day and your hat keeps flying off of your head! Chase it down and put it back each time, until finally you just throw it to the ground and walk away!

_____ /2

SILLY SCENARIOS TOTAL: _____ /4

TIME TO SCORE YOUR POINTS! →

/8

ROUND TOTAL

/8

ROUND TOTAL

ROUND CHAMPION

ROUND 2

Jokes

Why did the astronomer attend the Oscars?

He enjoyed star gazing.

/1

Why wouldn't the clothespins let the towels play on their team?

They knew they'd fold in a pinch.

/1

How do computers keep their nails short?

Files.

/1

Where do your toes keep their money?

Piggy Banks.

/1

JOKES TOTAL: /4

GOOBER 1 CONTINUE TO THE NEXT PAGE →

Silly Scenarios

(Act it out!)

It is the biggest blizzard in the history of the world, and you have to walk home from school. It is windy, snowy, freezing cold, and the snow is up to your belly! BRRR!

_____ /2

Your mom has asked you to mop the floor and to make it more fun you've decided to wear rollerskates. Try to finish mopping while slipping and sliding all over!

_____ /2

SILLY SCENARIOS TOTAL: _____ /4

NOW, PASS THE BOOK TO GOOBER 2 →

Jokes

What do you shout before you throw someone a pen?

"Ink-coming!"

/1

What is a chair's favorite type of clothing?

The seat belt.

/1

The Dorito's are kind of stingy. They never want to chip in!

/1

When is first aid boring?

When you have to use a bland-aid.

/1

JOKES TOTAL: /4

GOOBER 2 CONTINUE TO THE NEXT PAGE →

Silly Scenarios

(Act it out!)

You are in an intense swordfight but your sword is way too big for you. Keep fighting, but you have to use both hands to even pick the sword up!

_______ /2

You need to tell your family that your train is leaving in 30 minutes, but you can only communicate using your hands, face, and bird noises!

_______ /2

SILLY SCENARIOS TOTAL: _______ /4

TIME TO SCORE YOUR POINTS! →

/8

ROUND TOTAL

/8

ROUND TOTAL

ROUND CHAMPION

ROUND 3

Jokes

What comes out of the vents in a prince's or princess' bathroom?

The Air to the Throne.

_____ /1

Why did the jeweler love baseball?

Because it's played on a diamond!

_____ /1

What do you call a robot pirate?

"ARRGH2-D2."

_____ /1

The dragon is such a good rapper. He always spits FIRE!

_____ /1

JOKES TOTAL: _____ /4

GOOBER 1 CONTINUE TO THE NEXT PAGE →

Silly Scenarios

(Act It out!)

You're a ballerina practicing for tonight's recital. As you try to start spinning, you go spinning out of control, then throw up everywhere! It's a disaster!

/2

This year, Santa has asked that all Christmas lists are submitted in the form of interpretive dance. Go ahead and get your list ready!

SILLY SCENARIOS TOTAL: ______ /4

NOW, PASS THE BOOK TO GOOBER 2 →

Jokes

Why did the brain start a company by himself?

He was minding his own business.

/1

Why doesn't Winnie the Pooh wear pants?

He prefers to show his bear legs!

/1

Why did the baseball player go to his house?

The coach told him to run all the way to home!

/1

What's a tree's favorite game to play?

'Wood You Rather?'

/1

JOKES TOTAL: /4

GOOBER 2 CONTINUE TO THE NEXT PAGE →

Silly Scenarios

(Act it out!)

You're training to be a firefighter, but when the water hose is turned on it's SO strong! Do you best to get it under control as it pulls you in every direction!

_____ /2

You are a robot in Santa's workshop, but your wires got snow on them and now you're smashing all the toys!
(Tip: Don't forget to use robot noises!)

_____ /2

SILLY SCENARIOS TOTAL: _____ /4

TIME TO SCORE YOUR POINTS! →

/8

ROUND TOTAL

/8

ROUND TOTAL

ROUND CHAMPION

ROUND 4

Jokes

Why did the chef keep his burrito recipe a secret?

He didn't want to spill the beans!

______ /1

Why did the bee stop getting invited to parties?

He was a real buzz kill.

______ /1

What did the cop say to the sleeping man?

"You are under a REST!"

______ /1

What do you call a dancing cow?

A Milkshake!

______ /1

JOKES TOTAL: ______ /4

GOOBER 1 CONTINUE TO THE NEXT PAGE →

Silly Scenarios

(Act it out!)

You are a very upset child throwing a dramatic temper tantrum. Don't forget all the mean and sad faces you can use!

______ /2

You are at the top of a giant rollercoaster! Put your hands up and enjoy while you ride the twists and turns all around the room! Woohoo!!

______ /2

SILLY SCENARIOS TOTAL: ______ /4

NOW, PASS THE BOOK TO GOOBER 2 →

Jokes

What happens when Dumbo gets dizzy?

He ele-faints!

_____ /1

How did the tugboat relieve his gas?

He let out a little toot!

_____ /1

What is a gorilla's favorite fruit?

An APE-ricot.

_____ /1

How did the cows get their furniture to their new home?

They hired a MOO-ving company!

_____ /1

JOKES TOTAL: _____ /4

GOOBER 2 CONTINUE TO THE NEXT PAGE →

Silly Scenarios

(Act it out!)

Act like an inchworm cleaning the floor. You can't use any limbs to move around!

____ /2

Your shoe is stuck in the strongest gum in the world, and the bus is about to drive away without you! To get the driver's attention, make your wildest faces, do your craziest dance moves, but all while keeping one foot stuck to the ground! How do you manage to get unstuck?!

____ /2

SILLY SCENARIOS TOTAL: ____ /4

TIME TO SCORE YOUR POINTS! →

/8

ROUND TOTAL

/8

ROUND TOTAL

ROUND CHAMPION

ROUND 5

Jokes

What's another word for a name tag worn on your shirt?

Collar ID.

_____ /1

How do locomotives prepare for a competition?

They train!

_____ /1

Why was the basketball player so sad?

He lost his last quarter!

_____ /1

What animal do you call when your car breaks down?

A toad (towed).

_____ /1

JOKES TOTAL: _____ /4

GOOBER 1 CONTINUE TO THE NEXT PAGE →

Silly Scenarios

(Act it out!)

Try to cook a full breakfast while hopping on only one foot and also spinning in circles!

_____ /2

You wake up to discover your ears hang all the way to the floor. Tie them in a knot, throw them over your shoulders, wear them as a scarf - anything to get them out of your way!

_____ /2

SILLY SCENARIOS TOTAL: _____ /4

NOW, PASS THE BOOK TO GOOBER 2 →

Jokes

What do you call a personal bouncer for your teeth?

A Mouth Guard!

___ /1

Why isn't Cinderella any good at baseball?

Because her coach is a pumpkin!

___ /1

What do you call a one-year-old pouring water all over your head?

A Baby Shower!

___ /1

What did the dog say to the tree?

"I like your bark."

___ /1

JOKES TOTAL: ___ /4

GOOBER 2 CONTINUE TO THE NEXT PAGE →

Silly Scenarios

(Act it out!)

You're a crazy, starving monkey that escaped from the Zoo. You spot someone nearby eating a banana for lunch...Sneak over, grab the banana, and RUN!!!

_____ /2

You are a zombie that eats human brains. The only problem is - even though you have to eat them to survive, they totally gross you out! EW!

_____ /2

SILLY SCENARIOS TOTAL: _____ /4

TIME TO SCORE YOUR POINTS! →

/8

ROUND TOTAL

/8

ROUND TOTAL

ROUND CHAMPION

ROUND 6

Jokes

What did everyone in the family of pants have in common?

Their jeans (genes)!

____ /1

What do you call a question mark with a bad attitude?

'Punk-tuation.'

____ /1

What do you get when you cross a hockey player and a cow?

Ice cream!

____ /1

How can you tell if a mermaid farted?

It smells fishy!

____ /1

JOKES TOTAL: ____ /4

GOOBER 1 CONTINUE TO THE NEXT PAGE →

Silly Scenarios

(Act it out!)

Make a snow angel in the freshly fallen snow, but when you try to get up, you're frozen to the ground! No matter how hard you try, you can't seem to get yourself unstuck!

_____ /2

Act like a werewolf that just ate something REALLY spicy! Start howling and eating/ drinking anything to make the burn go away!

_____ /2

SILLY SCENARIOS TOTAL: _____ /4

NOW, PASS THE BOOK TO GOOBER 2 →

Jokes

Why can a yard stick run faster than you?

Because it has 3 feet.

____ /1

What do farmers use to write?

A pig pen!

____ /1

What do you call a bear who works at a coffee shop?

A BEAR-ista!

____ /1

What is a kangaroo's favorite restaurant?

IHOP.

____ /1

JOKES TOTAL: ____ /4

GOOBER 2 CONTINUE TO THE NEXT PAGE →

Silly Scenarios

(Act it out!)

You are a King/Queen relaxing on your throne. You take off your crown, kick up your feet, and take a sip of pretend wine. However, the wine was poisoned and now you have to die a DRAMATIC death!

______ /2

You are a star football player that just scored a touchdown! Time for a celebration! Show the crowd your best touchdown dance, but the ball is still stuck to your hand!

______ /2

SILLY SCENARIOS TOTAL: ______ /4

TIME TO SCORE YOUR POINTS! →

/8

ROUND TOTAL

/8

ROUND TOTAL

ROUND CHAMPION

ROUND 7

Jokes

How do worms get their energy in the morning?

GROUND coffee!

/1

What do you call a fancy mom?

A GRAND-mother!

/1

What do you call a pet that ate too much cotton?

A Stuffed Animal!

/1

What do kids who pick their nose, eat at McDonald's?

Hand-boogers.

/1

JOKES TOTAL: /4

GOOBER 1 CONTINUE TO THE NEXT PAGE →

Silly Scenarios

(Act it out!)

You're looking for a bathroom because you REALLY need to go! Do your best impression of the potty dance!

______ /2

You are a little hamster and just got out of your cage! Now run all around the room with your giant hamster cheeks and look for a way out!

______ /2

SILLY SCENARIOS TOTAL: ______ /4

NOW, PASS THE BOOK TO GOOBER 2 →

Jokes

What did the driftwood say to the seaweed?

"Ever feel like you're all washed up?"

_____ /1

What kind of parties do snowmen avoid?

Housewarming parties!

_____ /1

Why is it easy to open a candle shop?

All you need is common scents.

_____ /1

Why did everyone want to live next door to Mr. Horse?

Because he was such a good NEIGH-bor!

_____ /1

JOKES TOTAL: _____ /4

GOOBER 2 CONTINUE TO THE NEXT PAGE →

Silly Scenarios

(Act it out!)

You're trying to put together a puzzle, but the birds keep stealing your puzzle pieces and flying away. Use your lasso to capture the birds and retrieve the missing puzzle pieces!

______ /2

You reach into your backpack to grab a book, but instead, you grab a big, hairy spider! Freak out, jump, and shake your hand to GET IT OFF!!!

______ /2

SILLY SCENARIOS TOTAL: ______ /4

TIME TO SCORE YOUR POINTS! →

/8

ROUND TOTAL

/8

ROUND TOTAL

ROUND CHAMPION

ROUND 8

Jokes

Why is it hard for bell families to have conversations?

Someone is always chiming in!

_____ /1

Why didn't the tree ever leave their hometown?

Because they didn't want to abandon their roots!

_____ /1

Why did the farmer love his orchard?

Together, they made a perfect pear.

_____ /1

What is a dog's favorite place in City Hall?

Barks and Recreation.

_____ /1

JOKES TOTAL: _____ /4

GOOBER 1 CONTINUE TO THE NEXT PAGE →

Silly Scenarios

Goober 1

(Act it out!)

You decided to lay down in the park for a nice a nap, but you suddenly wake up to a burning feeling on your leg, now your other leg, and now your back! It's EVERYWHERE! You are covered in fire ants and they are biting you all over. Act out getting them off by slapping, rolling, jumping, whatever you can think of!

______ /2

You are a mime trapped in a giant invisible box. Do everything you can to get someone to help, but without making a sound.

______ /2

SILLY SCENARIOS TOTAL: ______ /4

NOW, PASS THE BOOK TO GOOBER 2 →

Jokes

How do you protect your eyes from bad jokes?

Put on your PUN-glasses!

______ /1

What city has the most courageous rocks?

Boulder.

______ /1

Why did the puppy always sit at the front of the class?

She was the teacher's pet!

______ /1

Why did the airplane fail as an actor?

Winging it was all he knew!

______ /1

JOKES TOTAL: ______ /4

GOOBER 2 CONTINUE TO THE NEXT PAGE →

Silly Scenarios

(Act it out!)

You're eating a juicy hamburger, but when you bite into it all of the fillings spill out on your lap! Pick them back up and put them back in the burger to finish your delicious meal!

_______ /2

Maraca master do your thing! You are the funkiest maraca player in the Mariachi band. Shake those shakers!!

_______ /2

SILLY SCENARIOS TOTAL: _______ /4

TIME TO SCORE YOUR POINTS! →

/8

ROUND TOTAL

/8

ROUND TOTAL

ROUND CHAMPION

ROUND 9

Jokes

Why did the kettle corn have so many friends?

It was really POP-ular!

_____ /1

Why did the tree go home early?

He had to LEAF.

_____ /1

What do you call kids who are always relaxed?

CHILL-dren.

_____ /1

What did the trout write on the postcard to his family?

"Fish you were here!"

_____ /1

JOKES TOTAL: _____ /4

GOOBER 1 CONTINUE TO THE NEXT PAGE →

Silly Scenarios

(Act it out!)

You are the world's most famous rockstar! Give your greatest air guitar solo yet!

_____ /2

Your alien spaceship just crash landed on Earth! Speak your alien language and try to make friends with the first human you see! But instead of shaking hands, you shake everything!

_____ /2

SILLY SCENARIOS TOTAL: _____ /4

NOW, PASS THE BOOK TO GOOBER 2 →

Jokes

What singer do aliens love most?

Bruno Mars!

/1

What dinosaur always gives it their best shot?

The TRY-ceratops!

/1

Where do gifted, young pigs go to school?

HOG-warts!

/1

What's the nun's favorite baseball team?

The Angels.

/1

JOKES TOTAL: /4

GOOBER 2 CONTINUE TO THE NEXT PAGE →

Silly Scenarios

(Act it out!)

You are a Superhero but are feeling very sleepy. Struggle to put on your tights, suit, and cape. Do you have enough energy to fly and fight the bad guys?

_____ /2

As a weatherman, you are in the middle of an important update when you suddenly feel like you're being tickled all over. Try to continue doing the weather report without laughing too much!

_____ /2

SILLY SCENARIOS TOTAL: _____ /4

TIME TO SCORE YOUR POINTS! →

/8

ROUND TOTAL

/8

ROUND TOTAL

ROUND CHAMPION

ROUND 10

Jokes

Which part of the house is always looking at you?

The stairs.

____ /1

Why wasn't the pug chosen to be in the dog food commercial?

They thought he was PUG-ly.

____ /1

What do you call a container of dynamite?

A Boom Box!

____ /1

What is the national anthem of monkeys?

The Star-Spangled Banana.

____ /1

JOKES TOTAL: ____ /4

GOOBER 1 CONTINUE TO THE NEXT PAGE →

Silly Scenarios

(Act it out!)

You find a beehive in a tree and start poking it with a stick. Suddenly, a swarm of bees flies out and starts chasing you! Slap them and run away to save yourself from their stingers!

_____ /2

You're a kangaroo at a dance party. Suddenly, the DJ plays your favorite song! Do your best impersonation of a dancing kangaroo!

_____ /2

SILLY SCENARIOS TOTAL: _____ /4

NOW, PASS THE BOOK TO GOOBER 2 →

Jokes

What do you call a lightbulb family reunion?

A flash mob!

/1

What state needs the most tissues?

Mass-Achoo!-setts.

/1

Why was the banana salesman so polite?

He had good nanners!

/1

Did you hear about the flower who came back to life?

It ROSE from the dead!

/1

JOKES TOTAL: /4

GOOBER 2 CONTINUE TO THE NEXT PAGE →

Silly Scenarios

(Act it out!)

You're a famous chef who makes the BEST pizza. Prepare the dough, flip it in the air, and catch it as you make your world famous pizza!

_____ /2

You're a baby bird competing with your siblings for food: open your mouth the widest, chirp the loudest, and flap your little wings for attention!

_____ /2

SILLY SCENARIOS TOTAL: _____ /4

TIME TO SCORE YOUR POINTS! →

/8

ROUND TOTAL

/8

ROUND TOTAL

ROUND CHAMPION

ROUND 11

TIE-BREAKER

ADD UP EACH PLAYER'S SCORE FROM ALL PREVIOUS ROUNDS. IF POINTS RESULT IN A TIE, MOVE ON TO THE TIE-BREAKER ROUND.

GRAND TOTAL

GRAND TOTAL

Jokes

What do you call it when a computer makes a joke?

A Giggle-byte.

_____ /1

What piece of furniture looks just like his brother?

A twin bed!

_____ /1

What's the iPhone's favorite sports team?

The Chargers.

_____ /1

Why did the poison ivy get a therapist?

It was acting ir-RASH-ional!

_____ /1

JOKES TOTAL: _____ /4

GOOBER 1 CONTINUE TO THE NEXT PAGE →

Silly Scenarios

Goober 1

(Act it out!)

You are an evil-genius, madman. You take pride in your long, boisterous laughs. Show everyone (use lots of arm motions)!

_____ /2

You are walking along barefoot on a hot sunny day and you notice that the pavement is getting hotter and HOTTER. Try to find some grass or a place to cool your feet down quick!

_____ /2

SILLY SCENARIOS TOTAL: _____ /4

NOW, PASS THE BOOK TO GOOBER 2 →

Jokes

What's a puppy's favorite potato chip?

RUFF-les!

/1

What do you call it when a bunch of hunter's get together?

A MEAT-ing!

/1

Why didn't the burrito like his date?

He didn't get to taco lot.

/1

Why was the family worried about camping?

Because it's IN-tents.

/1

JOKES TOTAL: /4

GOOBER 2 CONTINUE TO THE NEXT PAGE →

Silly Scenarios

(Act it out!)

You have magically transformed into a dog. Suddenly, your tail looks like it would be fun to catch! You bark and chase your tail round and round, but it keeps getting away!

______ /2

Someone else is controlling your arms and legs with strings like a puppet, making you dance the 'Hokey Pokey'!

______ /2

SILLY SCENARIOS TOTAL: ______ /4

TIME TO SCORE YOUR POINTS! →

ADD UP ALL YOUR POINTS FROM THE PREVIOUS ROUND. THE GOOBER WITH THE MOST POINTS IS THE ULTIMATE DON'T LAUGH CHALLENGE MASTER!

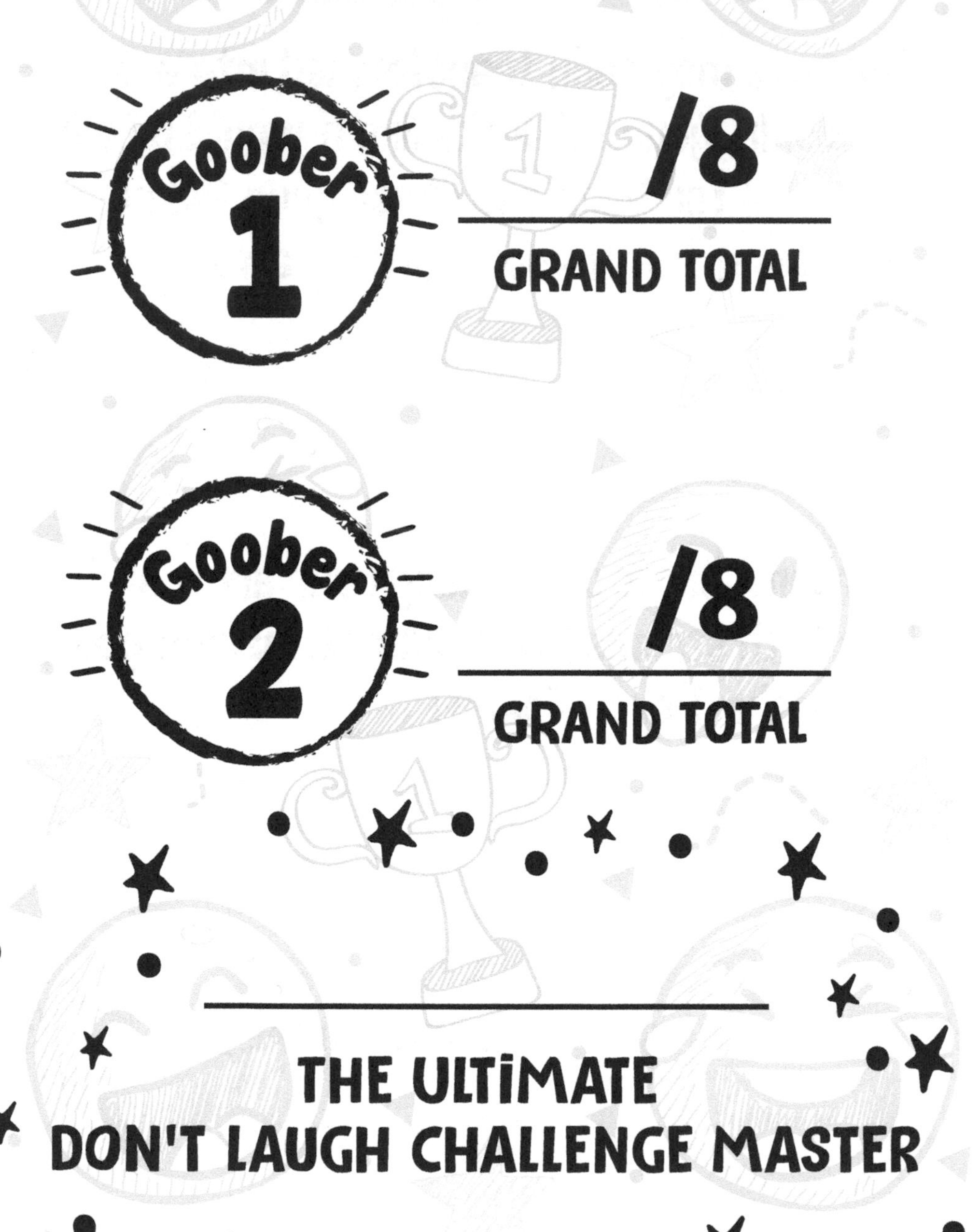

Check out our other joke books!

Visit us at

www.DontLaughChallenge.com

to check out our newest books!"